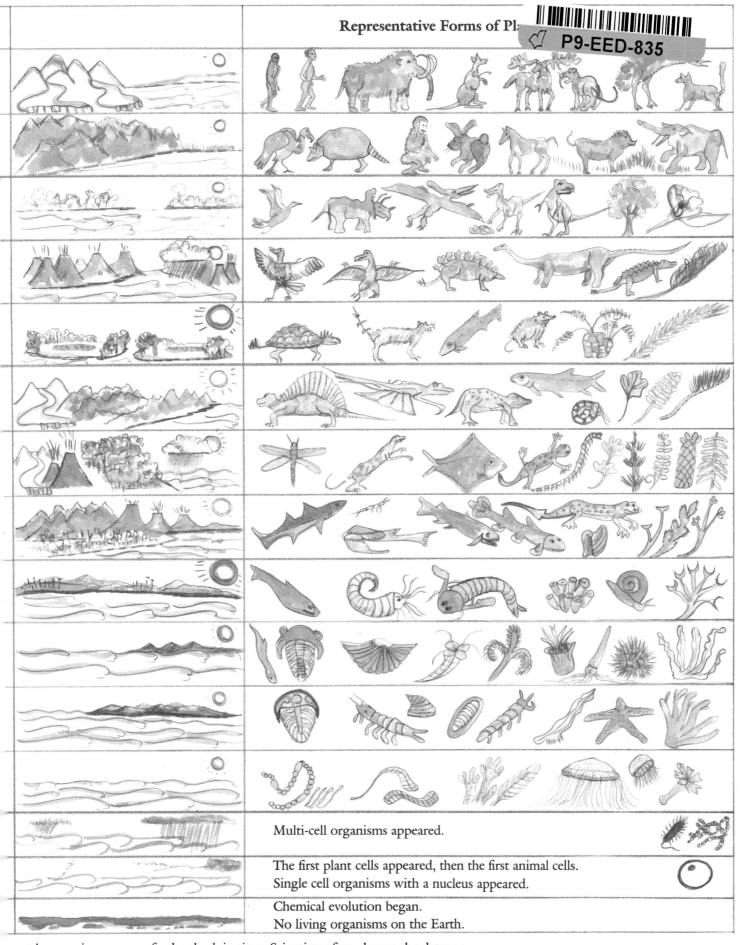

Multi-cell organisms appeared.

The first plant cells appeared, then the first animal cells.
Single cell organisms with a nucleus appeared.

Chemical evolution began.
No living organisms on the Earth.

get less precise as we go further back in time. Scientists often change the dates as
our dating techniques improve and new information is discovered.

Long, long ago, before you or I explored her shores, Earth was a much different place. In fact, 250 million years ago, Earth had only one continent, instead of the seven we know today. This was the mother continent of Pangaea (pan-GEE-ah), which in Greek means "all Earth."

Alfred Wegener, an early twentieth-century scientist, gave Pangaea her name. Then he spent his life trying to prove that this single supercontinent existed long ago and then split apart.

Why else, he reasoned...

...do the edges of South America and Africa fit together so well, like two pieces of a jigsaw puzzle? Why else are fossils of the same extinct plants and animals found on continents oceans apart? Why else do rocks from far away shores look so much alike?

Wegener saw only one answer to all three questions. He declared that millions of years ago all the continents must have been together as one — Pangaea. Then they drifted apart.

Many other scientists only laughed at Wegener's idea. To them, Pangaea was nothing more than a land in a fairytale.

Then in the late 1950s, nearly thirty years after Wegener's death, new information made people realize that he was right.

Pangaea *did* exist and this is her story.

Harbinger House, Inc.
Tucson

Project Director, Linnea Gentry

Text Copyright © 1989 by Karen Liptak
Illustrations Copyright © 1989 by Susan Steere

Published by Harbinger House, Inc., 3131 N. Country Club, Suite 106, Tucson, Arizona 85716.
Typesetting by Typecraft, Inc., Tucson.
Printed in Singapore by Singapore National Printers, Ltd. through Palace Press.

Library of Congress Cataloging in Publication Data

Liptak, Karen.
  Pangaea: the mother continent / by Karen Liptak; illustrated by Susan Steere.
    p.   cm.(Harbinger House juvenile natural history series)
  Bibliography: p.   Includes index.
  Summary: Traces the history of the earth's land forms and plant and animal life, from the first emergence of land masses to the beginning of the Cenozoic era approximately sixty million years ago.
    ISBN 0-943173 36-1: $15.95—ISBN 0-943173-42-6 (pbk.): $8.95.
    1. Pangaea (Geology)—Juvenile literature. [1. Pangaea (Geology)   2. Geology.]
    I. Steere, Susan, 1941– ill.   II Title.   III.Series.
  QE511.5.L57   1989   551.7'2—dc20   89-15495

We wish to give our special thanks to Dr. Peter Coney (Univ. of Arizona) and Dr. Ellis Yochelson (Smithsonian Institution) for reviewing the manuscript of this book and giving us a wealth of information and helpful suggestions.

The author and artist wish to thank their editor, Linnea Gentry, for her vision, patience, and creative direction.

PANGÆA
THE
MOTHER CONTINENT

by Karen Liptak
illustrated by Susan Steere

HARBINGER HOUSE JUVENILE NATURAL HISTORY SERIES

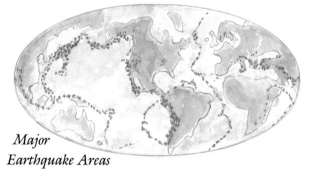

Major Earthquake Areas

Scientists had known for many years that Earth is formed like a set of globes nesting one inside the other. The core is on the inside, an outer core surrounds that, a mantle surrounds the outer core, and a thin crust is on the very outside.

During the past twenty-five years, earth science has been revolutionized by what is known as the **theory of plate tectonics**. ("Tectonics" refers to the movements of Earth's crust.)

According to this theory, Earth's crust is divided into about twenty sections, or "plates." The continents and oceans are passengers on these plates. When the plates move, which they are constantly doing, their cargo of land and ocean moves, too.

Scientists are just starting to learn about the forces deep within Earth that cause them to move. But we already know that plate material can be created as well as destroyed.

Plate material is created at great cracks in the seafloor called **rifts**. Scientists discovered the first of these rifts in the middle of the Atlantic Ocean in 1958. They have discovered others since then. Through these rifts, Earth belches forth hot liquid rock, called **magma**. This magma eventually becomes new crust.

Plate material is destroyed at the edges of the plates when an oceanic plate comes up against a continental plate. Ocean crust is heavier than continental crust. When these two plates meet, the ocean plate sinks and dives below the lighter continental plate. The ocean plate then melts into magma and becomes recycled into the mantle. Sometimes, where there are cracks on Earth's surface, the magma breaks through and causes volcanoes to erupt.

When two plates with continents collide, neither sinks. Instead, the land on both sides moves in the only direction possible: straight up! These squeezes create

SEAFLOOR SPREADING

RIFT

SEAFLOOR

CONTINENTAL PLATE

PLATE

COLLISION ZONE

OUTER MANTLE

INNER MANTLE

MAGMA

OUTER CORE

4

MAGMA

CORE

mountain ranges. The mighty Himalayas were forced into being millions of years ago when India rammed into Asia, leaving seashells up on Earth's highest peaks.

Sometimes two plates grind against each other without actually colliding. If the plates scrape with a jerk along their boundary (called a **fault**), an earthquake "hits." Such grinding action is going on right now along the San Andreas fault in California. There, the Pacific plate is traveling northwest beside the westward-moving North American plate.

How long have Earth's plates been on the move? Nobody knows for sure. However, scientists believe that when Earth first formed some 4.6 billion years ago, it had no land at all, no sea, no life. The newborn planet was nothing more than a chunk of solar debris in the heavens. But that was soon to change.

Earth is made up of many elements, such as oxygen, silicon, carbon, nitrogen, and hydrogen. Other rare elements, like uranium, are **radioactive**. Over time, radioactive elements break down, or "decay." Such decay causes heat.

Scientists think that over many millions of years, the decay of these radioactive elements inside Earth created enough heat to melt the interior rocks to magma for the first time. The magma oozed upward through the mantle. Wherever there were cracks in the crust, the magma broke through in the first volcanic eruptions of lava.

Gases from inside escaped to the surface along with the magma and eventually formed Earth's first atmosphere. Water vapor from this early atmosphere rained down in warm showers. Gradually the rains produced Earth's first oceans.

Still more magma poured out like taffy. Wherever it piled up high enough, chunks of black volcanic rock (the first true "earth" rock) broke through the early waters.

But no birds sang yet. No flowers bloomed. There was no life at all on the third planet from the Sun. Yet it was only a matter of time until life evolved.

SPREADING

MATERIAL

SUBDUCTION ZONE

RETURN OF
SEAFLOOR
TO MANTLE

MAGMA

EDITOR'S NOTE: The first time a scientific term appears in this book we have put it in **bold face type**. Where the Latin name of a plant or animal is used, it appears in *italic type*. Where the common name is used, it appears in normal roman type.

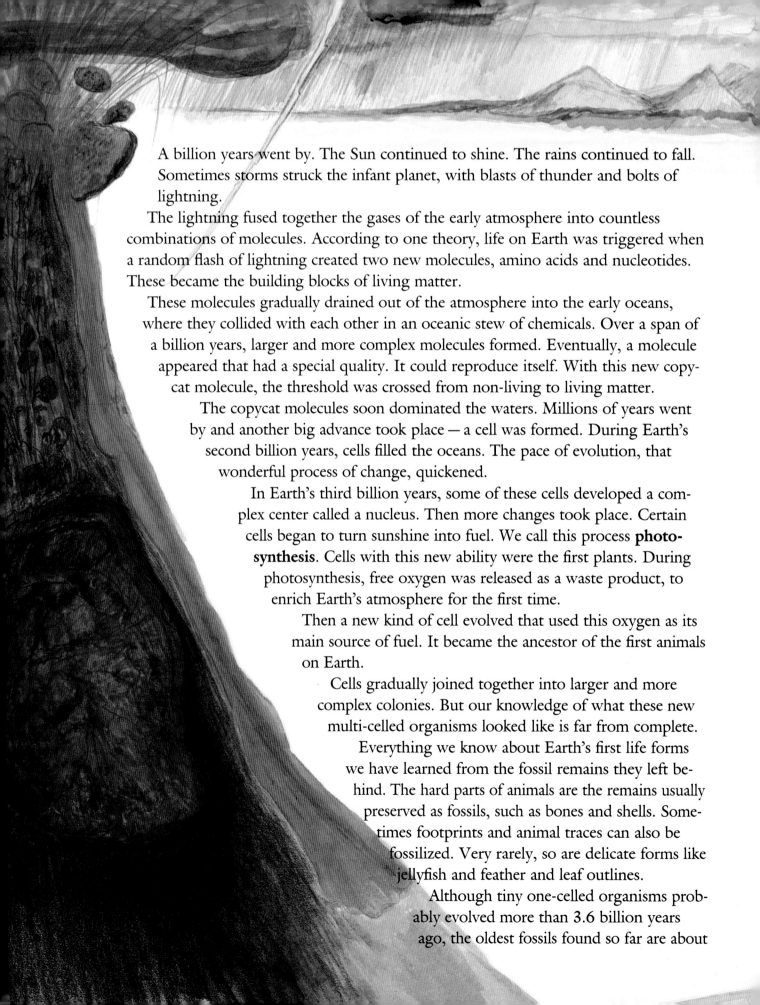

A billion years went by. The Sun continued to shine. The rains continued to fall. Sometimes storms struck the infant planet, with blasts of thunder and bolts of lightning.

The lightning fused together the gases of the early atmosphere into countless combinations of molecules. According to one theory, life on Earth was triggered when a random flash of lightning created two new molecules, amino acids and nucleotides. These became the building blocks of living matter.

These molecules gradually drained out of the atmosphere into the early oceans, where they collided with each other in an oceanic stew of chemicals. Over a span of a billion years, larger and more complex molecules formed. Eventually, a molecule appeared that had a special quality. It could reproduce itself. With this new copycat molecule, the threshold was crossed from non-living to living matter.

The copycat molecules soon dominated the waters. Millions of years went by and another big advance took place — a cell was formed. During Earth's second billion years, cells filled the oceans. The pace of evolution, that wonderful process of change, quickened.

In Earth's third billion years, some of these cells developed a complex center called a nucleus. Then more changes took place. Certain cells began to turn sunshine into fuel. We call this process **photosynthesis**. Cells with this new ability were the first plants. During photosynthesis, free oxygen was released as a waste product, to enrich Earth's atmosphere for the first time.

Then a new kind of cell evolved that used this oxygen as its main source of fuel. It became the ancestor of the first animals on Earth.

Cells gradually joined together into larger and more complex colonies. But our knowledge of what these new multi-celled organisms looked like is far from complete. Everything we know about Earth's first life forms we have learned from the fossil remains they left behind. The hard parts of animals are the remains usually preserved as fossils, such as bones and shells. Sometimes footprints and animal traces can also be fossilized. Very rarely, so are delicate forms like jellyfish and feather and leaf outlines.

Although tiny one-celled organisms probably evolved more than **3.6 billion years** ago, the oldest fossils found so far are about

2.5 billion years old. The oldest multi-celled animals known are 680 million years old. From these fossils, we know that some of Earth's earliest inhabitants were marine creatures, such as sponges and jellyfish. They are all **invertebrates**, soft-bodied animals with no backbones. No doubt other creatures also existed that have vanished without a trace.

According to the fossil record, by 600 million years ago, the first hard-bodied creatures had appeared. These include ancestors of the clam, the starfish, and the lobster.

Then about 510 million years ago, the earliest **vertebrates**, animals with backbones, appeared. These were fishes with only one fin on each side of the body, rather than the two fins which modern fishes have. They also had no jaw. Instead, they had a slit for a mouth.

When the first fishes emerged, the most plentiful creatures alive were tough sea creatures known as **trilobites** (TRY-lo- bites). These animals, the earliest thought to have eyes, are **arthropods** (AR-thro-pods), which means "jointed feet" in Greek. Today, this group includes crabs, shrimps, lobsters, centipedes, and insects.

The terrors of these early waters were the scorpion-like **eurypterids** (yoo-RIP-te-ridz). They were the largest arthropods ever to exist. Eurypterids grew up to 2.3 meters long (7 feet, 4 inches). They could even bite through the armor-plated bodies of the early fishes.

The deadly eurypterids, the bottom-dwelling trilobites, and the jawless fishes were not to last forever. Nor would the black volcanic chunks of rock above the sea stay barren forever.

Some 415 million years ago, the early landmasses in the Southern Hemisphere had already come together into the giant continent we call Gondwana (gon-DWAN-ah). It consisted of what are now South America, Africa, Antarctica, Australia, and India. And it was on Gondwana that another major advance took place. The first plants came ashore.

These moisture-loving mosses and liverworts probably descended from green sea algae that were stranded on land. While most of this algae dried out and died, the toughest plants managed to survive. But they could never be far from water. Lacking roots, leaves, and veins, they ringed the rocks with inviting necklaces of green and reproduced by spores.

For about 35 million years, these plant pioneers had the land to themselves. Then company arrived. Simple arthropods such as millipedes and scorpions became the first animals to scuttle across Earth's sandy shores. Evolution's pace sped up once more. And Pangaea, the mother continent, was just over the horizon.

Eurypterus

Stylonurus

Chiton

Lecanospira

Straparollus

Pliomera
(trilobite, curled up)

Bothriocidaris

Bellerophon

Charnia (sea pen)

7

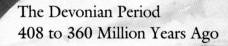

The Devonian Period
408 to 360 Million Years Ago

By the time Pangaea was starting to form some 400 million years ago, continental landmasses had probably existed for 2 billion years. Weathering was certainly taking place on them. Wind, water, chemicals, and ice crumbled up rocks and sculpted the land. Very likely, earlier barren supercontinents had already existed and broken apart.

As Pangaea's story continues, Earth is in her Paleozoic Era, which began 600 million years ago. Eras are major segments of time on Earth. Each era is divided into smaller units of time called periods. The Devonian is the fourth period of the Paleozoic Era.

Two great continents existed at this time. Gondwana, in the Southern Hemisphere, was the place where life on land first got its big break. Laurasia (lor-A-zha), in the Northern Hemisphere, had formed when the two large landmasses that are now North America and Europe bumped into each other, closing forever the ancient Iapetus (i-AP-eh-tus) Ocean between them.

North America and Europe cemented their union with a new mountain range. Today, remains of that range exist an ocean apart. In northeast North America they are the Appalachians. In northwest Europe they are the Caledonians.

Meanwhile, Gondwana was moving north, pushing smaller landmasses ahead of it. Now it was separated from Laurasia only by a narrow sea that was shrinking every year. This sea was named Tethys (TEH-thys), after the mother of the seas in Greek mythology.

What is today Central Africa lay over the South Pole, making it much colder than it is now. And the equator cut through what is now Canada. Our present-day North America was often flooded by shallow seas. Such floods left behind many marine fossils for sharp-eyed fossil hunters to find today.

As for the climate, it was warm and dry almost everywhere. Seasonal droughts were not uncommon. Scientists believe that these droughts helped bring about the next major advance in life on land: the arrival of the **amphibians**.

Cladoxylon

Psilophyton

Marchantia

Drepanophycus

Serpula

Conularia

Fucus

A RIVER FLOWS INTO THE SEA

But before amphibians made their debut, fishes had their fling. While Laurasia and Gondwana inched closer and closer together to form Pangaea, many kinds of fishes multiplied everywhere. They earned the Devonian its popular name of the "Age of Fishes."

Starting about 395 million years ago, jawless fishes shared the waters with their descendants, jawed fishes. Although the earliest jawed fishes developed in the sea, they eventually thrived in fresh water as well, replacing jawless fishes wherever they went. Why were jawed fishes so much more successful than their predecessors?

Fishes without jaws used up a lot of energy in eating, since they had to filter their food from the water through their slit-like mouths. Most of them cruised slowly on the bottom. Fishes with hinged, moveable jaws could eat a wider variety of food more quickly. This gave them more energy. Some were even able to eat the deadly eurypterids.

In the seas around the growing mother continent, jawed ancestors of our current sharks and rays preyed upon marine animals, like the trilobites and the ancient molluscs.

But the real drama of the day was taking place on the land.

By now the early land plants included **vascular** plants. A vascular plant has an interior pumping system to transport moisture and nutrients up from the ground. *Cooksonia* (cook-SON-ia) was the first known vascular plant. Its forked, leafless stems ended in a cup filled with spores. From this tiny plant, without roots and leaves, came Earth's first forests.

If you had been alive back then, you might have spied the first insect among groves of scale trees, horsetails, and feathery tree ferns. This little creature measured only 1 centimeter long (1/2 inch) and sported a prong under its tail. When alarmed a spring propelled the prong, sending the insect flipping into the air. Its common name is the springtail.

Unfortunately, fishes could not avoid danger so easily. Sometimes their freshwater pond or river dried up during a drought or the water became stagnant. What was a fish to do? It had to get to a fresh body of water fast! But to do this, a fish had to breathe air. It also required a method of transportation. Limbs were needed!

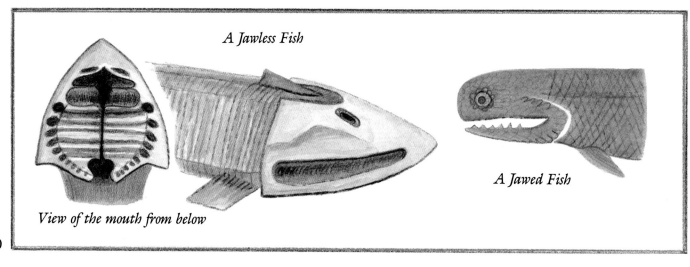

A Jawless Fish

View of the mouth from below

A Jawed Fish

A Eusthenopteron (a fleshy finned fish) crawls ashore, startling springtails in a patch of Cooksonia. An Ichthyostega remains in the water.

Eventually, a new group of bony fishes developed lungs for breathing air. Foremost among them were the fleshy-finned fishes. Their improved muscular fins enabled them to "walk" on land. (Actually, it was more like crawling.) From them, the first four-footed animals evolved. These were the amphibians.

But amphibians were still tied to the water. In fact, the word "amphibian" in Greek means "those with two lives." Although an amphibian can walk on land, it must lay its eggs in water. Otherwise the embryo (young animal) inside the egg will dry up. An amphibian's skin presents another problem. In general, it cannot retain moisture for a long period of time. The animal must always return to its other life in the water.

At present, the oldest amphibian we know about is *Ichthyostega* (IK-the-o-STE-ga), a Devonian inhabitant of what is now Greenland. Amphibians thrive in warm climates with plenty of water. Therefore, we can safely say that today's ice-covered Greenland was a much warmer place 350 million years ago. In fact, back then Greenland was located over the equator.

The fossils of *Ichthyostega* show that it still had fishlike features. Most likely, it was a clumsy walker with small, weak limbs and a heavy, stumpy trunk. Just the same, it left its mark as the first amphibian on the evolving continent of Pangaea.

11

The Carboniferous Period
360 to 286 million years ago

Meganeura

Lepidendron (Scale tree)

Sigilleria

Stylocalamites

Calamites (Horsetail)

Microbrachis

By 360 million years ago, the great continents of Laurasia and Gondwana were almost touching, with only a narrow strip of the Tethys Sea between them. Warm, moist weather and widespread, lush swamplands created a golden age in which the amphibians thrived. In fact, the Carboniferous is nicknamed the "Age of Amphibians."

In North America, this period is divided in half. During the first part, called the Mississippian, warm seas covered much of what is now North America. Limestone, a kind of rock made of the remains of dead sea creatures, was created in abundance. Today, Mississippian limestone is one of the best places for fossil hunting. The arthropods, corals, molluscs, and other creatures that flourished in the shallow seas can still be found beautifully preserved today. So can the flower-like animals on stalks known as sea lilies, or **crinoids** (CRY-nodz). So many crinoids were found in Mississippian limestone, that this part of the Carboniferous is also called the "Age of Crinoids."

Following North America's Mississippian period came the Pennsylvanian period. The seas began a restless cycle of retreat and return.

The landscape was graced with scale trees as much as a hundred feet tall. Tree ferns and horsetails also grew higher than ever before. When the shallow seas swept across the growing continent of Pangaea, all vegetation was drowned out. But when the seas retreated, new swamplands grew. Fossils of these forests make up most of the coal beds of central and eastern North America, China, Europe, and other parts of the world.

Meanwhile, the slow collision of Laurasia and Gondwana caused remodeling around the globe. North America's southern Appalachians rose up, as did the ancestral range of the Rockies and the Ouachitas of Arkansas.

Canobius

Dorypterus

Lichen

Blattidae (Cockroaches)

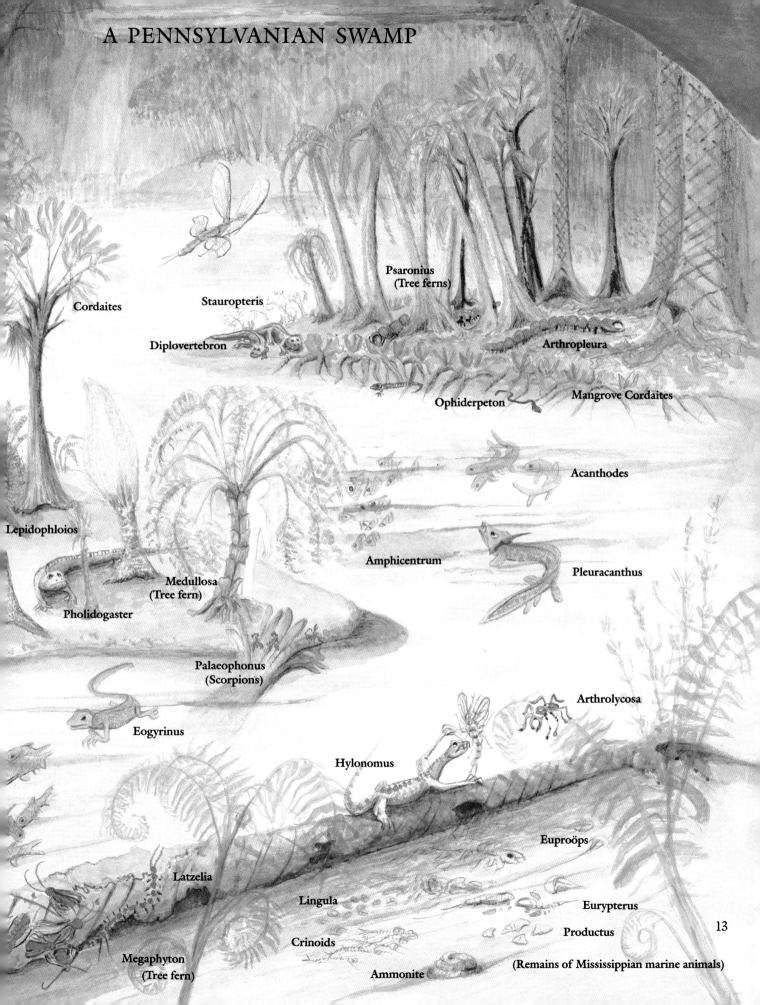

A PENNSYLVANIAN SWAMP

Cordaites

Stauropteris

Diplovertebron

Psaronius
(Tree ferns)

Arthropleura

Ophiderpeton

Mangrove Cordaites

Lepidophloios

Acanthodes

Medullosa
(Tree fern)

Amphicentrum

Pleuracanthus

Pholidogaster

Palaeophonus
(Scorpions)

Arthrolycosa

Eogyrinus

Hylonomus

Euproöps

Latzelia

Lingula

Eurypterus

Productus

13

Megaphyton
(Tree fern)

Crinoids

Ammonite

(Remains of Mississippian marine animals)

A cotylosaur leaps for some passing Meganeuras.

All kinds of land arthropods, including new winged insects, enjoyed the menu served in this cafeteria of swampland delights. Seed ferns made their entrance here. They looked like spore-producing ferns, but they reproduced by an entirely new method: seeds. Another early seed producer was the tall slim ancestor of conifers known as the **Cordaite** (KOR-dite) tree. Later in our story, we shall see why seed reproduction was so great an advance.

Arthropods dined on the plants and also on each other. In turn, they provided a rich food supply for many amphibians. While bulky amphibians stayed in the murky swamp waters, the smaller, more nimble ones chased insects on land. A real prize for the day must have been *Meganeura* (meg-ah-NUR-ah), the largest insect that ever lived. This giant dragonfly had a wingspan of about 75 centimeters (30 inches)!

But the life of a quick little amphibian was not all fun and games. When they returned to the water — as return they must — they risked being eaten by their larger relatives, as well as by large fishes.

Some scientists theorize that it was the constant struggle to eat, yet not be eaten, that led to a new kind of animal. It would be able to hunt down the juiciest prey on land without having to return to the perilous waters ever again.

The **cotylosaurs** (KOT-il-o-sawrs) fit the bill nicely. They are Earth's first reptiles and seem to have appeared about 280 million years ago.

Reptiles differ from amphibians in many ways. Most importantly, a reptile reproduces with a new kind of egg, one that can be laid out of water. (We'll get to the egg later on.) Furthermore, a reptile's scaly skin can hold in moisture. At last, after animals had evolved for millions of years, Earth had her first true land vertebrate.

The little cotylosaurs that merrily chased the biggest insects of all time (including cockroaches larger than jumbo crayons) are also known as "stem reptiles." All other reptiles stem, or have developed, from the cotylosaurs. Tiny turtles, dinosaurs two stories tall, crocodiles, and cobras — all can trace their ancestry to these three-foot-long creatures with sharp teeth, long tails, and pointed snouts. Equally impressive, cotylosaurs are believed to be the stem from which today's birds and mammals come.

Since humans are mammals, that makes the little cotylosaur your relative, too!

MAKING COAL

About half of the twentieth-century's usable coal reserve comes from the unique swamps of the Carboniferous period. As the shallow seas flooded the swamps and then withdrew over and over again, these giant plants were often buried without completely rotting.

After millions of years, the pressure of numerous layers of semi-rotted plants created a soft, fibrous substance called peat. After many more millions of years and many more mass burials, the pressure of these layers squashed, or "compressed," the peat into coal. Today, discoveries of coal deposits deep below Antarctica's frozen surface tell us that this icebox of a continent had a much warmer past.

GLACIATION

There have been many episodes of ice ages on Earth. During these times of **glaciation,** sheets of solid ice cover much of the globe. Temperatures plunge well below normal. Sea water gets locked up in ice and sea levels drop. At the same time, the weight of the ice forces the land beneath it to sink.

Although most people think of the Carboniferous as a time of swamps, a major ice age actually began at the end of this period and lasted for 10 to 25 million years. Like all ice ages, this one shaped the land, grinding down older mountains and carving out new peaks. Ice smothered all of Antarctica, as well as parts of Australia, South America, Africa, and India.

The future of Earth's plants and animals was also shaped by the ice. Only those able to adapt to the changing conditions would survive.

15

Ginkgo

The Permian Period
286 to 248 million years ago

Change was in the air. As Earth's multi-million-year chill continued, reptiles gained the evoutionary edge over amphibians. In time, the reptiles would become the undisputed masters on Pangaea.

The two great continents of Laurasia and Gondwana were now together. All of Earth's land was one, with perhaps a few islands here and there. Around the mother continent was a mammoth ocean named the Panthalassa (pan-tha-LAS-ah). A sliver of the ancient Tethys Sea pierced Pangaea between Africa and Asia.

When the Permian period opened, the Southern Hemisphere was still under the icy thumb of glaciation. Bitter cold was everywhere. But as Pangaea drifted northward, the glaciers nearing the equator began to melt.

Whenever glaciers retreated, lands that had been weighted down by the ice rose up again. At the same time, sea water was released, overflowed onto the land, and then retreated again until more ice melted. These cycles of flooding caused erratic weather, which ranged from freezing cold to blistering heat. Since the amphibians depended on warm, moist climates, they could not endure such changes as well as the reptiles could.

Moschops

Pangaea was "growing up" now. Her landscape began to change as well as her climate. Rolling hills and great mountains formed in many places, especially in the Northern Hemisphere. Ranges that later became the Alps in Europe and the Urals in the USSR (Union of Soviet Socialist Republics) were pushed up.

The west coast of today's United States was dotted with volcanoes, while the western interior was primarily hot and dry. Many deposits of sandstone stained red by iron were in the making. Such deposits are now called "red beds."

Dimetrodon

Here was the super landmass of Wegener's dreams: Pangaea, the place where plant and animal life exploded in so many forms. Had you wandered through the Permian forests, you might have passed by many of the now extinct plants and animals that Wegener made famous. He used them to prove that his theory of Pangaea and drifting continents had to be right.

Bug

Beetles

AN INLAND RIVER

Conifers

Weigeltisaurus

Psaronius

Edaphosaurus

Calamitana

Eryops

Scutosaurus

Mesosaurus

Palaeoniscum

Diadectes

Lycosuchus

Diplocaulus

Ophiacodon

(Remains of Carboniferous marine animals)

Phthinosuchus

Cicada

Eunotosaurus

Seymouria

Araeoscelis

Venyukovia

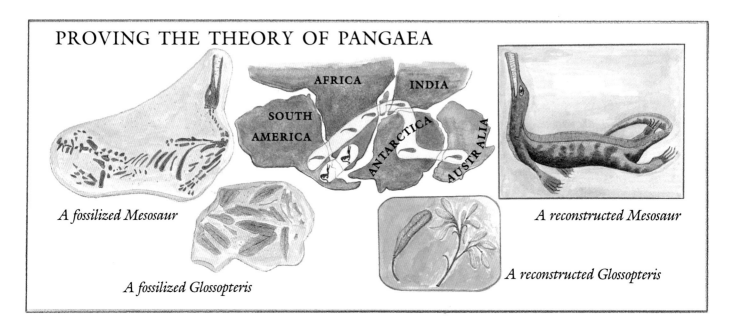

PROVING THE THEORY OF PANGAEA

AFRICA
INDIA
SOUTH AMERICA
ANTARCTICA
AUSTRALIA

A fossilized Mesosaur

A fossilized Glossopteris

A reconstructed Mesosaur

A reconstructed Glossopteris

The picture above shows two fossils Wegener used as examples. *Glossopteris* (glos-OP-ter-is) was one of the earliest seed plants. This **gymnosperm** (JIM-no-sperm), or "naked seed" plant, had large leaves and a delicate rib system. Its fossils have been found thousands of miles apart on separate continents. Wegener reasoned that its seed was much too heavy to be carried these great distances by the wind. Therefore, the lands had to be much closer together in the past.

As for *Mesosaurus* (mez-o-SAWR-us), fossils of this marine reptile have been discovered in both South America and South Africa. However, it seems to have favored the fresh or slightly salted water of lakes and rivers. This makes it highly unlikely that *Mesosaurus* traveled across the entire Atlantic Ocean. The only logical explanation, argued Wegener, is that the continents must have once been together and then drifted apart.

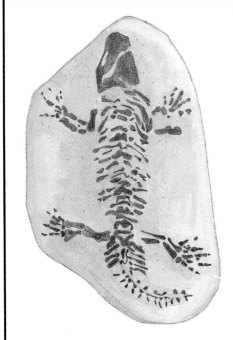

THE MYSTERIOUS SEYMOUR

The fossil record is as full of gaps as it is full of contradictions. For instance, meet *Seymouria* (see-MOR-e-ah), a walking sideshow of a character whose name comes from the town near where this fossil was first found: Seymour, Texas. Some scientists classify *Seymouria* as a cotylosaur reptile. Others consider it to be a **labyrinthodont** (lab-e-RIN-tho-dont) amphibian. This large group of amphibians survived until 180 million years ago. They were named for the maze-like (labyrinth) structure of their teeth. Some had weak skeletons and lived in water. Others, like the 60-centimeter-long (2-foot) *Seymouria*, developed strong backbones, strong limbs, and lived on land.

But *Seymouria* didn't have to return to the water to lay eggs, like true amphibians did. Fossils show that it laid the same kind of egg as the reptiles!

In all, *Seymouria* had 10 amphibian features , 2 fish features, and 11 reptilian features. What do you think it was?

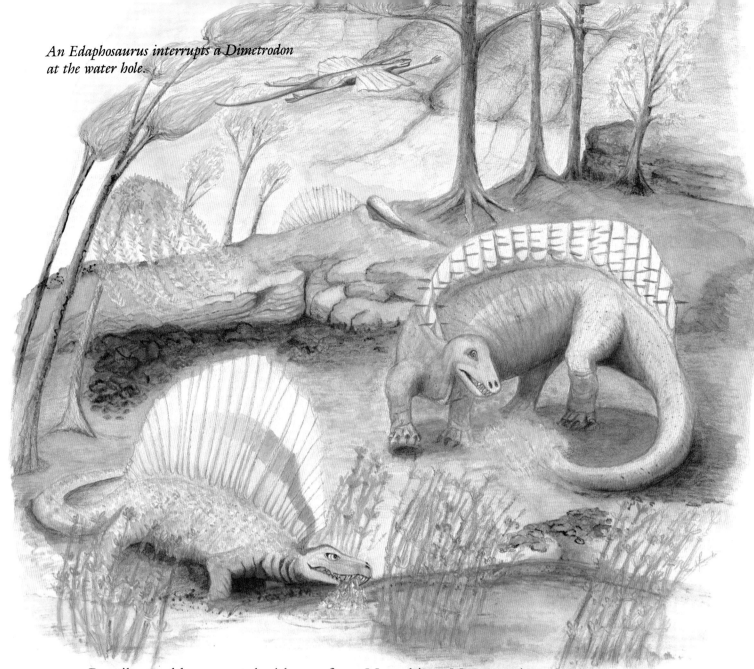

*An Edaphosaurus interrupts a Dimetrodon
at the water hole.*

Reptiles could now travel with ease from Memphis to Moscow, since there were no seas to stop them. They spread out, multiplying everywhere. During the first part of the Permian, no reptile was more successful nor more spectacular than the **pelycosaurs** (pe-LIC-o-sawrs).

Often mistaken for dinosaurs, which they are not, pelycosaurs were to have 35 million years of supremacy on Pangaea. Some of them had a magnificent fin supported by bones that ran up their back. In fact, these pelycosaurs were nicknamed "finbacks."

The meat-eating *Dimetrodon* (di-MEH-tro-don) measured about 3.5 meters long (11 feet, 6 inches) and had teeth as sharp as steak knives. Equally large was *Edaphosaurus* (e-DAF-o-sawr-us), a pelycosaur vegetarian with peg-shaped teeth well suited for chewing plants.

Today, scientists puzzle over the pelycosaurs' fins. What was their purpose?

Perhaps a clue comes from the fact that most reptiles, as well as amphibians, fishes, and insects, are cold-blooded. They can't adjust their body temperature internally like mammals and birds can. Cold-blooded animals depend on their surroundings for their temperature.

19

With this point in mind, some scientists suggest that the pelycosaur's fin was a heat regulator. When it was cold, they warmed up by turning sideways to the sun, so their fins absorbed the heat. When they were too hot, they cooled off by turning their backs to the sun, so their fins lost heat.

Other scientists think that the fins were for defense, since they made the animals look larger and more frightening than they really were. Still others think that the fins were for attracting pelycosaurs of the opposite sex and may even have been beautifully patterned. But though bones become fossils, skin is almost never preserved. So we can only guess at the truth. This is just one more mystery encountered when studying animals now extinct.

The intriguing therapsids (the-RAP-sidz) are the descendants of rather plain-looking, finless pelycosaurs. They are known as "mammal-like reptiles," because they seem to lead directly to early mammals.

Although some were bulky and slow vegetarians, most therapsids were active meat eaters, ranging in size from a mouse to a bear. Their skeletons were generally lighter than those of other reptiles. Also unlike amphibians and other reptiles, the therapsids' limbs were almost directly under their bodies, perpendicular to the ground like a mammal's limbs. This made them very speedy animals.

Moschops (MO-shops), a large therapsid (2.8 meters, or 8 feet long) with a huge ridge on its skull, was probably a peaceful vegetarian, judging by the peg-like teeth.

Lycosuchus (ly-co-SUKE-us) was a meat-eating theriodont (THER-i-o-dont), or "mammal-toothed" therapsid. All meat-eating therapsids had specialized teeth for ripping, cutting, and chopping their food, just as modern meat eaters do. Theriodonts went a step further. Their mouth and nasal passages were separated. This novel improvement let them breathe while eating, like mammals. Some scientists also suspect that these "mammal-toothed" therapsids may have been warm-blooded and hairy.

By the end of the Permian period, 85 percent of all reptiles on Pangaea were therapsids. And what about the pelycosaurs which preceded them? They became extinct.

They were not alone. The Permian ended with a mass extinction of many forms of life.

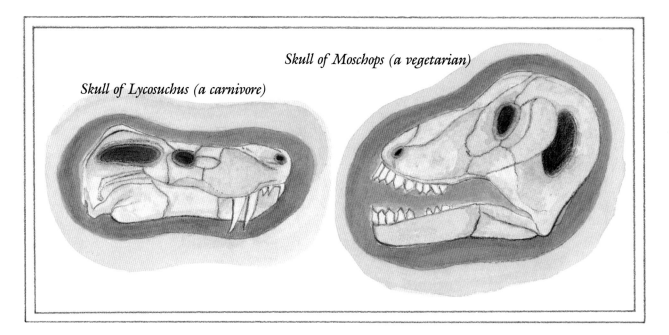

Skull of Moschops (a vegetarian)

Skull of Lycosuchus (a carnivore)

More plants and animals were lost during this mass extinction than at any other time.

Gone were most marine groups, including the once numerous trilobites and the frightening eurypterids. Gone were the fleshy-finned fishes that were the ancestors of the amphibians. Gone were many of the amphibians and reptiles.

Yet other amphibians and reptiles lived on. The lakes and rivers still teemed with bony fishes, many of which adapted to the sea. New insect groups which had recently emerged on Pangaea also survived. These were the early beetles, bugs, and cicadas whose descendants are with us today.

What could have caused so many life forms to die out, while others survived? So far, scientists don't agree on an answer. Yet one thing is sure. After this mass extinction, a mass explosion of new life repopulated the Earth.

THE SEED AND THE EGG: Two Better Ways to Reproduce

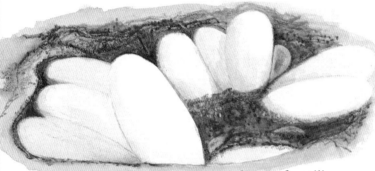
A nest of reptilian eggs

Both gymnosperm plants and reptilian animals became widespread in the Permian. Very likely, their means of reproduction had much to do with their success.

As you may remember, the seed ferns were the first gymnosperms, or "naked seed" plants. By the Permian, Pangaea was decorated with great forests of gymnosperms, including ancient pines and firs.

All gymnosperms reproduce in basically the same way. In pines, male sperm cells and female eggs are produced by the same tree. But the wind carries the sperms to other pines where they fertilize, or "enter," the egg cells. The fertilized egg then becomes a plant embryo. The embryo grows inside a seed coat that protects the future plant as the wind sweeps it away from the parent plant.

If conditions are right in its new resting place, the young plant will sprout and grow into a pine tree. Because of its protective coat, a gymnosperm has a much better survival rate than a spore-bearing plant.

What the gymnosperm was to plants, the new reptilian amniotic (am-ne-OT-ik) egg was to animals. Unlike the more fragile egg of the amphibian, this reptilian improvement is a sturdy, self-contained unit that can be laid on land. Within its tough shell a reptilian embryo has an efficiently packed food and water supply. Later on, this new egg would be produced by both birds and mammals.

The birth of a pine tree, from cone to sapling

21

The Triassic Period
248 to 213 million years ago

Plateosaurus

With the vast ice sheets in the south almost gone, Earth now entered an exciting new phase — the Mesozoic Era. This is also known as the "Age of Dinosaurs."

Once again, Pangaea was beginning to show signs of a continuously restless nature. Soon the continents of Laurasia and Gondwana would form again, with the narrow Tethys Sea between Asia and Africa.

Animals could still roam over much of the mother continent. But what are now South America and northwest Africa were being severed from North America by an ocean rift. Antarctica and Australia began to drift away from Africa. And India set out on what was to be a 5,000 mile journey northward.

Sea water overflowed many continental shores. From the fossils these floods left behind, we know that the first marine group to recover from the Permian extinction was the ammonites. Though these coiled sea creatures had just barely survived, they now spread rapidly.

Meanwhile, volcanic eruptions gave rise to the Palisades on what is now the east coast of the United States. Similar volcanic formations arose all over, especially on the western edge of what are now North and South America.

Plateosaurus
(Juvenile)

Changes in climate were less extreme. While you wouldn't have found colorful flowers or succulent grasses, Triassic forests of conifer trees, tree ferns, and cycads were probably pleasant places. Along waterways and in marshes, tall horsetails added still more greenery to the landscape.

The therapsids now shared the land with the **thecodonts** (THEE-co-donts). The teeth of thecodonts were set in sockets, unlike other reptiles whose teeth are set in the jaw. The dinosaurs come from a group of thecodont reptiles. So do the **pterosaurs** (TER-o-sawrs), or "flying reptiles," and the crocodiles. The remarkable crocodiles are the only reptiles alive today from this ancient dinosaur lineage.

Amia

In Triassic skies, you would have seen reptile gliders, the forerunners of the pterosaurs. In the seas, you would have marveled at a growing number of new marine reptiles.

Earth's recovery from the Permian extinction brought a rich variety of new plants and animals to Pangaea. Keeping track of them all is no easy task!

Saurichthys

A SHALLOW SEASHORE

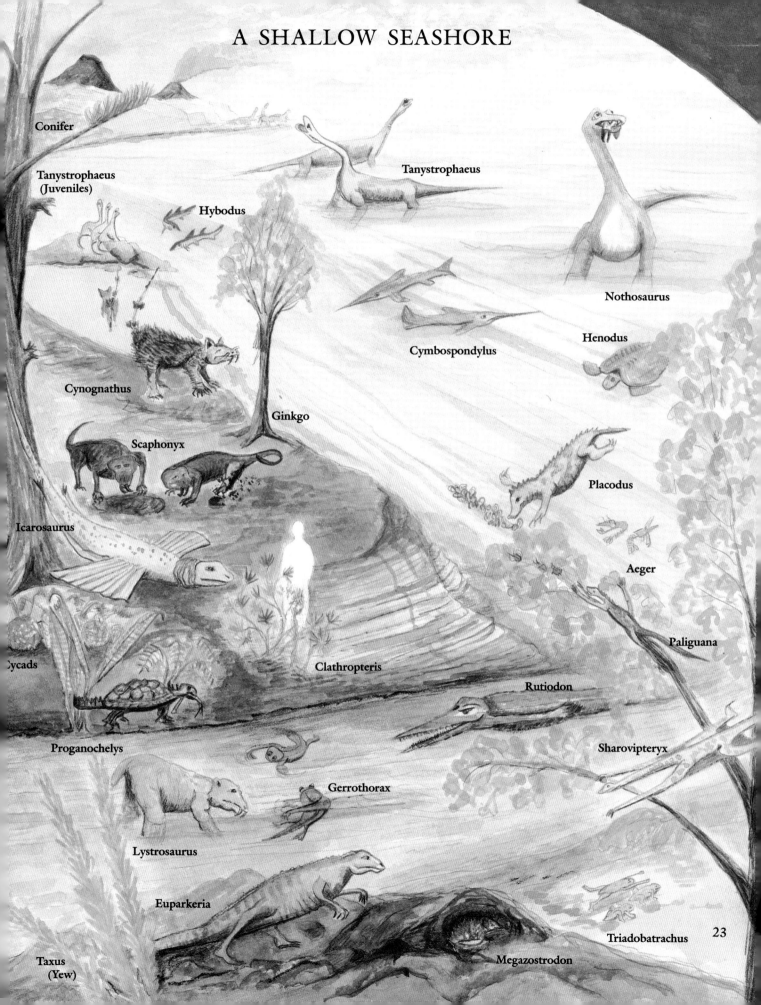

Conifer

Tanystrophaeus
(Juveniles)

Hybodus

Tanystrophaeus

Nothosaurus

Cynognathus

Cymbospondylus

Henodus

Ginkgo

Scaphonyx

Placodus

Icarosaurus

Aeger

Cycads

Paliguana

Clathropteris

Rutiodon

Proganochelys

Gerrothorax

Sharovipteryx

Lystrosaurus

Euparkeria

Triadobatrachus

23

Taxus
(Yew)

Megazostrodon

HOW WE ORGANIZE WHAT WE KNOW

As scientists in the eighteenth century learned more and more about life on Earth, they needed a way to organize all the new data. Today that need is greater than ever. Over three million species of living organisms are now known!

Two ways to make sense out of all these life forms are Carolus Linnaeus' **classification system** and **family trees**.

Linnaeus was an eighteenth-century Swedish naturalist who developed an ingenious method of classifying plants and animals. He grouped together all organisms, whether alive or extinct, by their similarities.

The groups are in a series where small groups are inside larger groups that are inside still larger ones. The largest group is the **kingdom**. All plants belong to the kingdom of *Plantae* and all animals belong to the kingdom of *Animalia*.

Animals are then put into smaller groups called **phylums** and plants into **divisions**. These are then divided into the smaller groups of **class**, **order**, **family**, **genus**, and **species**. Members of each group also belong to all the larger groups that come before. The species is the smallest group. Members of a particular species can breed together but not with any other species. Most of their characteristics are the same.

The River Cooter Turtle

Subspecies: *concinna*
Species: *concinna*
Genus: *Chrysemys*
Family: *Emydidae*
Suborder: *Cryptodira*
Order: *Testudines*
Class: *Reptilia*
Phylum: *Chordata*
Kingdom: *Animalia*

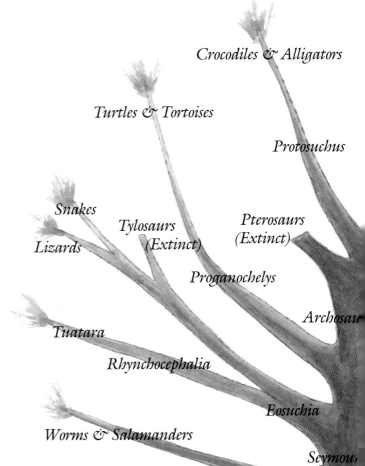

Crocodiles & Alligators

Turtles & Tortoises

Protosuchus

Snakes

Tylosaurs (Extinct)

Pterosaurs (Extinct)

Lizards

Proganochelys

Archosaur

Tuatara

Rhynchocephalia

Eosuchia

Worms & Salamanders

Seymour

Ichthyosteg

A good way to grasp how classification works is to take yourself as an example.

Like all animals, you belong to the kingdom of *Animalia*. Because you have a backbone, your phylum is *Chordata*. (You share this phylum with all mammals, reptiles, amphibians, birds, and most fishes.) Your class is *Mammalia*. Your order is Primates, which you share with monkeys, apes, lemurs, and tarsiers. Your family is *Hominidae*, which consists of human beings and our closest prehuman ancestors. Your genus is *Homo*, the Latin word for human being. Your species is *Homo sapiens*. Finally, you and every other person alive today belong to the subspecies of *Homo sapiens sapiens*, to separate us from the extinct subspecies of Neanderthal man.

It's a lot of information packed into one system. But keep in mind that scientists do not always agree on how certain plants and animals should be classified. (Remember *Seymouria*?)

Another method for keeping track of life forms is to group them on a "family tree." (Don't confuse this with the "family" level of Linnaeus' classification system.) Family trees show how one group of organisms may have developed into another. They indicate stems as well as branches in the evolutionary scheme of things. But there is a lot of information still unknown.

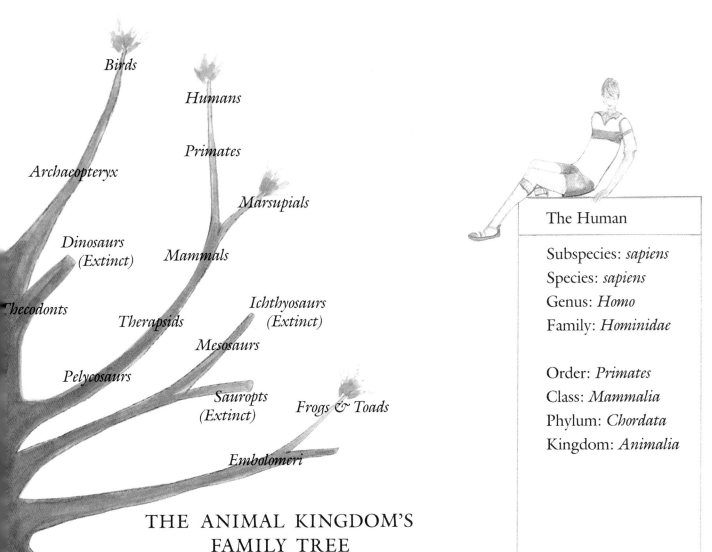

THE ANIMAL KINGDOM'S
FAMILY TREE

The Human

Subspecies: *sapiens*
Species: *sapiens*
Genus: *Homo*
Family: *Hominidae*

Order: *Primates*
Class: *Mammalia*
Phylum: *Chordata*
Kingdom: *Animalia*

Fossils of **ichthyosaur** (IK-thee-o-sawr), or "fish lizard," have been found around the globe. One of the first was discovered in 1812 by Mary Anning, a twelve-year-old girl looking for seashells on a beach in England. Mary went on to make many other important fossil finds when she grew up. Today, ichthyosaur is Nevada's state fossil. But 200 million years ago it was a lively marine reptile of the sea. Though its ancestors evolved on land, ichthyosaur's legs had changed into flippers to accommodate an aquatic life. Sleek and dolphin-like, it grew as long as 7.6 meters (25 feet) and gave birth to its young in the water.

Turtles and tortoises form one of the oldest living orders of reptiles. The early turtle *Proganochelys* (pro-gan-o-KEL-is) had teeth as well as a beak. It probably couldn't pull its limbs, tail, or head inside its shell as most turtles can today. But this little armored fellow needn't fear the curious dinosaurs. *Plateosaurus* (PLAY-tee-o-SAWR-us), one of the first giant dinosaurs, ate only plants. Their fossils have been found in Germany, Argentina, China, South Africa, and North America.

The trend was towards bigger reptiles everywhere. *Tanystrophaeus* (tan-i-STRO-fee-us) was a marine reptile who used its strange, long neck for fishing in the shallow seas. Its young appear to have lived on land until adulthood.

Yet in the shadows of the giant reptiles lurked another kind of animal: the first mammals. The rare fossils of these early mammals reveal small-eyed, furry, warm-blooded little creatures with long snouts and sharp ears. They were probably nocturnal. (The large eyes of today's nocturnal mammals was a later development.) They also nursed their young with milk produced from special glands, as mammals do today. From their remains, we know they were only a few inches long, about the size of mice.

Here were the new brains on the planet. Early mammalian brains seem small in comparison to mammalian brains today. But in the proportion of brain to body weight, early mammals far surpassed the dinosaurs. A dinosaur's brain was bigger in actual size,

A mother plateosaur and her youngsters stop to investigate a Proganochelys.

but the dinosaur had to use nearly all of its brain to control its huge body. The small mammal needed only a small part of its brain for body control. It had plenty left over for other tasks.

But why did the ancient mammals develop better brains in the first place? Perhaps the need to outwit the giant reptiles forced mammals like *Megazostrodon* (meg-ah-ZOS-tro-don) to use their brains for more complex thinking. Only the smartest escaped being a meat-eating dinosaur's dinner and lived to pass on the trait of intelligence to their offspring.

Here were the only descendants of the therapsids, the ruling mammal-like reptiles we met earlier. Meanwhile, for 140 million years, the mighty dinosaurs reigned.

A Megazostrodon ventures out into the moonlight.

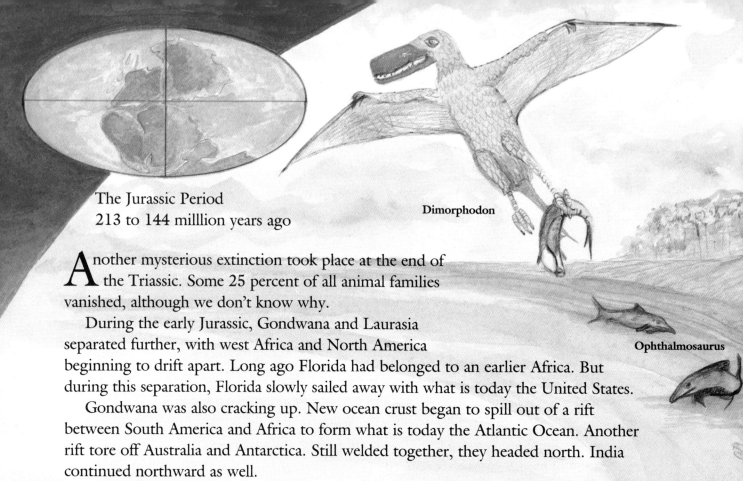

The Jurassic Period
213 to 144 milllion years ago

Dimorphodon

A nother mysterious extinction took place at the end of
the Triassic. Some 25 percent of all animal families
vanished, although we don't know why.

During the early Jurassic, Gondwana and Laurasia
separated further, with west Africa and North America
beginning to drift apart. Long ago Florida had belonged to an earlier Africa. But
during this separation, Florida slowly sailed away with what is today the United States.

Gondwana was also cracking up. New ocean crust began to spill out of a rift
between South America and Africa to form what is today the Atlantic Ocean. Another
rift tore off Australia and Antarctica. Still welded together, they headed north. India
continued northward as well.

Before long, Gondwana and Laurasia would divide further, leaving South America
as an island continent in the Southern Hemisphere. Yet in the early Jurassic there were
still enough connections between the continents for animals to wander across them
with ease. Very likely, they passed through forests of conifers that later created new
deposits of coal.

As for the climate? If dinosaurs could have sent postcards, they would have written
"the weather's great!" The dinosaurs shared warm, moist days with new amphibians
such as frogs and salamanders. New insects also appeared, including the ancestors of
today's wasps, ants, earwigs, flies, and caddis flies. Bees were here, too, although there
were still no flowers from which to gather pollen.

Among the new reptiles was the **tuatara** (too-ah-TAR-ah). This creature now lives
only in parts of New Zealand, which seems to have separated from Gondwana about
70 million years ago, with the tuatara on board. Isolated from many predators, the
tuatara went on to achieve fame as a living fossil, remaining practically unchanged
since its first appearance. But the unique little tuatara was rather unimportant
compared to other reptiles of the Jurassic.

In the seas, marine reptiles grew larger than ever. Among these were the
bizarre **plesiosaurs** (PLE-si-o-sawrs) with necks reaching 30 feet long. In the
skies were peculiar flying reptiles (the pterosaurs), as well as a new creature that
sported feathers: the earliest known bird. We can make a pretty good guess what
these fliers saw when they looked down on the land. Dinosaurs everywhere!

Ophthalmosaurus

Elasmosaurus

Peloneustes

Ichthyosaurus

28

ALONG A JURASSIC BEACH

Rhamphorynchus

Araucaria
(Monkey puzzle)

Williamsonia

Stegosaurus

Diplodocus
(Juvenile)

Brachiosaurus
(Juvenile)

Scelidosaurus

Apatosaurus
(Brontosaurus)

Aellopos

Eryon

Allosaurus
(Juvenile)

Thaumatosaurus

Protosuchus

Wasp

Belemnite

Proganochelys

Fly

Earwig

Allosaurus
(adult)

Homoeosaurus
(Relative of
the tuatara)

Bug

Karaurus
(Salamander)

Ants

Archaeopteryx

Cycad

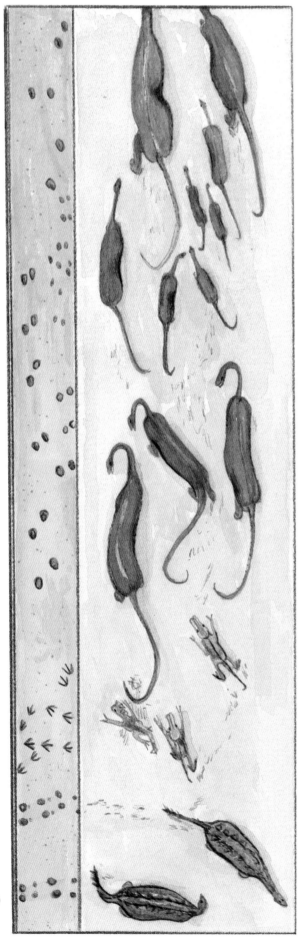

Dinosaurs left many footprints on Pangaea. Such footprints sometimes became fossils if they were made in soft mud and were quickly covered by sediment that hardened. They show that dinosaurs were not the slow, clumsy, solitary creatures we once thought them to be.

Track measurements reveal that some dinosaurs were very agile. Some of them traveled in herds with the adult dinosaurs on the outside, apparently to protect the youngsters in the middle. Some smaller, meat-eating dinosaurs ran in packs, like wolves do today. Such packs could bring down even the giant plant eaters like *Diplodocus* (dih-PLOD-o-kus), whose whiplike tail 26.6 meters long (87 feet!) earns him the record for dinosaur length.

Scientists classify dinosaurs in two main orders based on the shape of their hips. All dinosaurs were either **lizard-hipped** or **bird-hipped**.

According to the fossil record, the earliest dinosaurs were bird-hipped creatures about the size of a chicken. They walked only on their hind legs. Gradually they evolved into much bigger animals. To support their bulky bodies, many dropped down onto four feet instead of two. One of the earliest large bird-hipped dinosaurs was *Stegosaurus* (STE-go-sawr-us). This well-known fellow probably stood on its hind legs to graze on tree branches.

Later, bird-hipped dinosaurs would come in a variety of fantastic shapes, including duckbilled, horned, and boneheaded. All the bird-hipped group seem to have been vegetarians.

Not so the group of lizard-hipped dinosaurs. Among these were the ferocious *Allosaurus* (al-o-SAWR-us), a 35-foot-long meat eater with saber-sharp teeth, and the huge, infamous *Tyrannosaurus* (ty-RAN-o-sawr-us) of later times. This group also included the gentle giant *Diplodocus* and other vegetarians. Common to them all is their hip structure and enormous size.

A small pack of allosaurs threaten a herd of Diplodocus, while two stegosaurs move away.

Meanwhile, Pangaea's pterosaurs and early birds were testing their flying skills. The pterosaurs were fur-covered reptiles with wings that developed from the arms and "hands" of their ancestors. Three fingers were still used for clinging purposes, but the fourth finger now stretched out to support the pterosaur's large, skin-like wings. Their fossils have turned up on every continent but Antarctica.

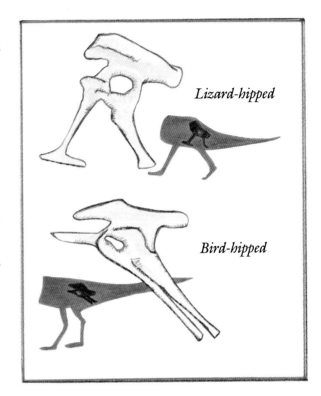

Lizard-hipped

Bird-hipped

Scientists are still not sure how the larger pterosaurs managed to leap into flight. Perhaps breezes carried them aloft from perches at the tops of cliffs, similar to the way a hang glider takes off. Once in flight, some seem to have soared on air currents, while others flapped.

Many scientists consider *Archaeopteryx* (ar-kee-OP-ter-iks), or "ancient wing," the first bird. Others think it's a kind of dinosaur. Fossil records show that *Archaeopteryx* had long feathers. Its bird wings are thought to have evolved from the hands of *Compsognathus* (komp-SOG-nah-thus), an early small, meat-eating dinosaur. Some scientists suggest that *Archaeopteryx* took off by climbing trees with their clawed limbs and then flapped their wings to maneuver down safely.

Both ancient flying reptiles and early birds had new lightweight skeletons that were streamlined for flight. Their hollow bones were filled with air pockets.

But why did pterosaurs die out, while birds lived on? Again, we can only guess. Perhaps birds survived because their feathers grow back after an injury. The skin wings of pterosaurs couldn't repair themselves. Then there's the difference in their legs. When a pterosaur's wing was damaged and it fell to the ground, its clumsy legs prevented it from running away from danger. But when a bird was grounded, its strong limbs gave it the chance to flee from predators and live on to reproduce. In the theory of evolution, being able to reproduce is basic. Otherwise your species dies out rather than evolves.

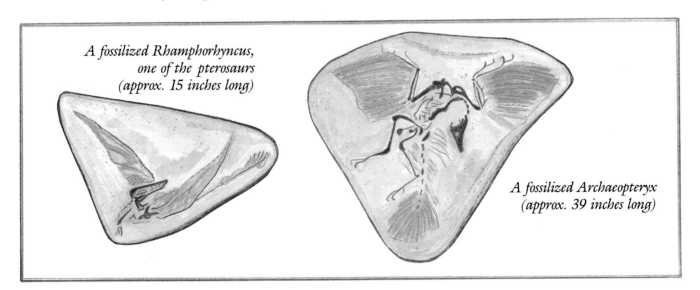

A fossilized Rhamphorhyncus, one of the pterosaurs (approx. 15 inches long)

A fossilized Archaeopteryx (approx. 39 inches long)

Tyrannosaurus

Pteranodons

Triceratops

Deinonychus

Maiasaura at her nest

The Cretaceous Period
144 to 65 million years ago

Nothing on Earth is as constant as change. Yet by 65 million years ago, the drifting continental fragments of Pangaea had nearly reached their present shapes and positions. Plate collisions were thrusting up the mighty mountain ranges of the Rockies in North America and the Andes in South America.

The ever-widening Atlantic Ocean was splitting Laurasia in half, with North America on one side and Europe and Asia on the other. Greenland became an island between them.

In the Southern Hemisphere, rifting in the Atlantic pushed South America and Africa further apart. At one point, sea water rose higher than ever before or since. Marine life flourished.

It was in Cretaceous breezes that the first flowers began to sway. Flowering plants are **angiosperm** (AN-gee-o-sperm), or "enclosed seed," plants. The angiosperm seed is sheltered in a container, such as a fruit, nut, or pod. This offers greater protection to its embryo than the seed coat of a gymnosperm. By 70 million years ago, 90 percent of all plants on Earth were angiosperms.

These early flowering plants, like magnolias and maples, were welcomed by Earth's pollinators. New butterflies, that seem to have evolved along with angiosperms, were busy now. So were buzzing bees, after millions of years without a petal in sight.

Many animals lived among the first blush of flowers. These included early snakes, new kinds of birds, and, of course, more fascinating dinosaurs.

Recent fossil finds are forcing scientists to form new theories about these gigantic inhabitants. We now know that some dinosaurs nested. But what kind of mothers were they? And were dinosaurs warm-blooded, like birds and mammals? Some scientists answer yes. They argue that only warm-blooded bodies would have the energy that speedy dinosaurs like *Deinonychus* (dyne-ON-i-kus) needed to run fast and survive in the cold climates where their fossils have been found. That raises a new question.

Dinilysia
(Boa-like)

Warmblooded animals living in very cold places have feathers or fur to help them stay warm. Were dinosaurs covered with feathers or fur?

Pterosaurs with fifty-foot wingspans swept over Cretaceous seas filled with giant reptiles and ammonites, as well as fishes and crustaceans that were much like those of today. The mammals probably continued to scurry about on land only at night.

But the mammals would not be in the dark forever. Sixty-five million years ago, the dinosaurs, pterosaurs, and big marine reptiles disappeared. So did the ammonites and many other groups.

Some scientists think that the mass extinctions were caused by a comet or asteroids that struck the Earth and drastically changed the climate. Others think that widespread volcanic eruptions were the cause. But they do agree on one point. The close of the Mesozoic Era marked the end of the world for the dinosaurs. At the same time, it marked the beginning of the world for another class of animals.

Soon the mammals would inherit the scattered pieces of Pangaea.

Ichthyornis
(Tern-like)

Bees

Teleost

Magnolia virginiana
(Swamp magnolia)

Butterfly

Protungulatum

Turtle

Zalambdalestes
(Rat-like)

Deltatheridium

33

With the dawn of the Cenozoic Era (which we are still in), Earth continued rearranging herself in many ways. Fifty to sixty million years ago, an oceanic rift divided Australia and Antarctica. This gave each continent the custody of plants and animals that developed in isolation from then on. Forty million years ago, India crashed into Asia.

Only two million years ago at the beginning of today's Quaternary period, South America and North America reunited. This took place at the Isthmus of Panama. Many animals that had evolved in isolation were free to mingle and compete. The Isthmus also separated the Atlantic and Pacific oceans — and their life forms.

Mammals spread rapidly over the post-Pangaean Earth. By two million years ago, the ancestors of today's dogs, bears, and horses had already appeared. In rock strata from that time, scientists found the first fossils they consider human enough to be given the genus name *Homo*. Our subspecies, *Homo sapiens sapiens*, appeared about 50,000 years ago.

Today, magma beneath the Atlantic Ocean creates new ocean crust that pushes North America and Europe apart at a rate of about an inch a year. In the Pacific Ocean, the seafloor is spreading at up to ten times that amount. The Pacific plate continues to grind

past the North American plate, threatening to surge forward before the next century and cause an even stronger earthquake than the San Francisco quake of 1906.

The African plate is slowly drifting north, shrinking the Mediterranean Sea, which was a dry valley just six million years ago. A rift is breaking East Africa off from the rest of the continent. The Himalayas are getting 5 centimeters (2 inches) taller each year. Australia maintains a steady northeasterly drift. It has already begun to collide with Indonesia. In time, a new mountain range may seal the union between them.

Perhaps in the distant future, *Homo sapiens sapiens* will somehow help guide Earth's plates in their natural movements. After all, look how far we've come in just 50,000 years! We have built oceanic research vessels, space satellites, and ground-based technology to expose the deepest secrets beneath Earth's land and seas. Scientists are even finding ways to predict earthquakes and volcanic eruptions. New discoveries by fossil sleuths and geological thinkers are constantly forcing changes in how we view the Earth of yesterday, today, and tomorrow.

Our planet's life story is an exciting puzzle that we are still piecing together. But perhaps we won't be the ones to finish the puzzle. In a few million years we may be extinct. Maybe a more adaptable species will replace us. Or we may have left Earth far behind by then, to inhabit other planets yet to be discovered circling some distant star. The possibilities are many.

And what about Pangaea, that pearl of the Permian-Triassic? Is she gone forever? Some scientists believe that many millions of years from now, a new Pangaea will form. Then all the continents will be one again, until new rifting begins new continental divisions.

There's a lot to wonder about as you sit on the beach, gazing out to sea. About how we got here...and where we're going.

But no matter which of Earth's mysteries you ponder, one thing seems certain. The ground beneath us will continue to drift on a planet both hot-hearted and beloved: Earth, the once and future home of Pangaea — The Mother Continent.

FOR FURTHER READING

Amphibians, in The History of Life on Earth series, by Giuseppe Minelli. Published by Facts On File Publications, New York. 1987.

The Audubon Society Field Guide to North American Fossils by Ida Thompson. Published by Alfred A. Knopf, New York. 1982.

Dinosaurs: An Illustrated History by Edwin H. Colbert. Published by Hammond Incorporated, Maplewood, N.J. 1983.

Dinosaurs Walked Here and Other Stories Fossils Tell by Patricia Lauber. Published by Bradbury Press, New York. 1987.

The Field Guide to Prehistoric Life by David Lambert and the Diagram Group. Published by Facts On File Publications, New York. 1985.

Giants of Land, Sea & Air: Past & Present by David Peters. Published by Alfred A. Knopf, New York, and Sierra Club Books, San Francisco. 1986.

The Life Nature Library, of which there are numerous titles (*The Reptiles, The Amphibians, The Birds, The Mammals, The Plants,* etc.) written by experts in each field and the editors of Life. Published by Time, Inc., New York, in the 1960s.

The Macmillan Illustrated Encyclopedia of Dinosaurs and Prehistoric Animals: A Visual Who's Who of Prehistoric Life by Dougal Dixon, Barry Cox, R. J. G. Savage, and Brian Gardiner. Published by Macmillan Publishing Company, New York. 1988.

INDEX

Eras	Millions of Years Ago	Periods and Their Meanings	Dominant Features of the Periods	
CENOZOIC	The present 2	QUATERNARY (The fourth foundation)	Climate is currently mild. Earlier, a great ice age occurred. Mammals are the dominant animals. Modern man appeared.	
	Lasted 63 million years 65	TERTIARY (The third foundation)	Climate was mainly mild. Great mountains were built. Continents reached their present locations. Grasslands developed. The first modern mammals, including primates, emerged.	
MESOZOIC	Lasted 79 million years 144	CRETACEOUS (Chalky)	Climate mostly warm or mild. Seas widespread. Thick chalk deposits formed. Flowering plants appeared. First modern trees spread. Dinosaurs with horns and armor. Modern insects and small mammals. Major mass extinctions at end of period.	
	Lasted 69 million years 213	JURASSIC (Named for the Jura Mountains in Europe)	Climate was warm and damp. Many active volcanoes. Continents began taking on their present shapes. Dinosaurs and marine reptiles thrived. Flying reptiles and the first birds appeared. Wasps, ants, and bees among the new insects.	
	Lasted 35 million years 248	TRIASSIC (Named for three layers of rocks in Europe)	Climate ranged from hot to mild. Large inland deserts. Pangaea starting to break up. The first dinosaurs and marine reptiles, along with the first turtles and crocodiles. The earliest mammals. Cycads. Mass extinctions at end of the period.	
PALEOZOIC	Lasted 38 million years 286	PERMIAN (Named for a town in the USSR)	At first, glaciers covered much of Southern Hemisphere. Later, melting ice made climate unstable. Pangaea now intact. Frequent mountain building. Life evolved rapidly. Reptiles and insects plentiful. Conifers. Period closed with major mass extinction.	
	Lasted 74 million years 360	CARBONIFEROUS (Coal-bearing)	Climate mostly warm and moist. Much volcanic activity. Major coal deposits. Amphibians abundant. Large arthropods, including giant insects. The first reptiles appeared. An ice age began at end of the period in the Southern Hemisphere.	
	Lasted 48 million years 408	DEVONIAN (Named for the English county of Devon)	Climate was warm and fairly dry. Much mountain building and volcanic activity. Widespread land vegetation began. Fishes with jaws spread. The first amphibians and the first flying insects appeared.	
	Lasted 30 million years 438	SILURIAN (Named for an ancient Welsh tribe)	Climate was warm. Deserts scattered globally. The first land plants and the first air-breathing land animals appeared. Fishes increased in number. Jawed fishes developed.	
	Lasted 67 million years 505	ORDOVICIAN (Named for an ancient Welsh tribe)	Climate was mainly warm. Seas often spread over much of the land. Sea animals and sea weeds dominated. The first vertebrates (jawless fishes) emerged. Trilobites remained the most numerous animals. Sea scorpions terrorized the waters.	
	Lasted 85 million years 590	CAMBRIAN (The Latin word for Wales)	Climate was mostly mild. The seas retreated at the end of the period. Plant and animal life was entirely marine. Algae were the dominant plants and trilobites were the dominant animals.	
	Lasted 80 million years 670	EDIACARIAN (Named for rocks in South Australia)	Free oxygen increased. Multi-celled organisms numerous. Then algae, worms, sponges, and jellyfish appeared.	
PROTERO-ZOIC	3,000		Continents were formed, then shaped by weathering. Iron formation widespread.	
EOPHYTIC	3,800		Earth's mantle being formed. Oceanic crust emerged.	
PREBIOTIC (Before Life)	4,600		No earth rocks known.	

Scientists date the time segments of Earth's history according to layers of rock.
Particular layers are laid down at particular times. Dates are approximate and they